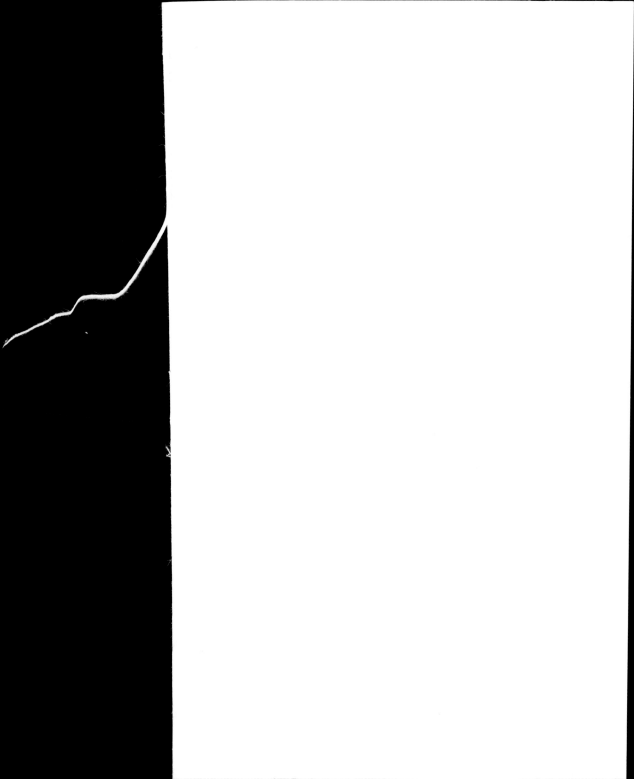

A
HINGE
OF SPRING

*Patience
Wheatley*

A HINGE OF SPRING   *Patience Wheatley*

4 - A

© Copyright Patience Wheatley, 1986

Published by Fiddlehead Poetry Books & Goose Lane Editions Ltd.,
Fredericton, New Brunswick, Canada, 1986, with the assistance of
the Canada Council and the University of New Brunswick.

Some of these poems have appeared in *The Antigonish Review,
Mamashee, Contemporary Verse II, Quarry, Origins, Grain, Northern Light*
and *Event*.

Cover design by Rebecca Leaman

Canadian Cataloguing in Publication Data

Wheatley, Patience, 1924-
    A hinge of spring

Poems.

I. Title.

PS8595.H43H5 1986   C811'.54   C86-093761-5
PR9199.3.W44H5 1986

ISBN 0-86492-076-8

1 THE WAY IN IS THE WAY OUT

7 Direction
8 The Way In is the Way Out
9 Sea Pool
11 Picking Raspberries with Gerda
12 Montreal from St. Catherine's Lock
13 Interiors
14 The Anatomist
15 Relax and Enjoy It
16 Quebec Painters
17 Circling
18 Casting Off — Thornhill Avenue, Montreal

2 JUST VISITING

21 Fishing for the Inuit Sea Goddess
24 Distances
25 Just Visiting
27 Black Hole
28 Outage at Key Biscayne
30 St. Helier, Jersey, Channel Islands
32 Zero Fahrenheit
33 At Birling Gap
34 Regatta at Portsmouth

3 A HINGE OF SPRING

37 Silver
38 Days Out
40 A Taste of Purdy
41 Home Thoughts from At Home
42 An Old Man's Spring
43 Bursting the Cocoon
45 We are Weeds
46 A Hinge of Spring
47 La Bête

4 *IS IT REALLY LOVE?*

51 Drought
52 The Passenger's Seat
53 Seaside Love Song
55 Is it Really Love?
56 Killed While Cleaning his Gun
57 City Love

5 *SHADOWS*

61 Warping Out
62 Her Room in Paris
64 Winter
65 Once an Imayo
66 Peepholes 1 — Glimpse
67 Peepholes 2 — Writing Fiction
68 Shadow of Icarus' Wing — for Jon
72 Tanka Very Much

1

THE WAY IN IS THE WAY OUT

DIRECTION

On the road from the
Bus Station,
tiered on the steps
of a red-doored church,
are seven black-
clad men.

I am
moored to a
red light
in the car
in a red sun . . .

Once at a red light
I saw two travellers
hugging and kissing.
And now
a voice hails me . . .
a motorist asking
the way.

At the Bus Station —
between my love and I —
nothing was
like an iceberg
except what lay below the surface . . .
It only exploded into view
at parting —
at the Bus Station —
when the ice rolled over
roiling all the deep water.

Follow the
route signs
I say,
casting off
my mooring.

THE WAY IN IS THE WAY OUT

I was older than the others
and walked into the laboratory
through the reek of decay and formaldehyde
shutting the door behind me

sunlight fell in rectangles
over rows of sheeted forms
and the bones of dangling skeletons
and the prosector
performing his last task
of dusting the tables
                              there
in cylindrical jars
pig-faced foetuses goggled
and students nudging past
set a bare brain quivering
                              was this
the soft coral where
Tennyson saw a blind life?
Eliot's multifoliate rose?

I joined the others beside the cadaver
and laid on its cloth-covered chest
scalpel, forceps, needle and scissors:

the first cut
was the putting together.

SEA POOL

Flint lights
flashing from
rippling rock
pond. My
finger is bent by sun-

light.   Its tip
finds   bottom
deep   cool   sand

_____

like a charged rod
activating iron filings
my finger gives life to

sandfleas and shrimps

_____

heavy on my white hat
/ the hammer sun /
salt-prickled skin
shrinks / eyes filter

sea-glitter / sand-dazzle

and all around irrepressible
pulse and swollen collapse
of each wave with a

hot rattle of shingle
and my finger / slides in
to / a quick-
sand of time

_____

and the sun
slams down /
and I'm falling
          under the wave

fish-mouthed
my mind opens and
shuts

—————————————

plovers cry / crabs squeak

—————————————

I jerk my finger

into air.

PICKING RASPBERRIES WITH GERDA

In the cavern of butterfly leaves
where flies drunk on ripe syrup swim
the warm blastulae
hang in still air
heavy, fulfilled, like old women with
big families, like young women with
milk-filled breasts

the raspberries fall into my waiting hand while
purple clouds behind me advance up the sky
deliberate spots of rain bend twigs
mark furrows until the thunder growls
like distant jets or the fleet of
fortresses I once saw filling
the silver dawn over Aldershot
intent on bombing Germans, smashing houses
juggernauting into the sunrise, majestic, beautiful
making our brutish round of tea and dirt bearable
deadening even the crunch of our feet
on the parade ground —
later, sewing cuddly toys for
orphans, imagining the laundries, signals,
casualty sections where we'd work
we heard the fortresses return with
low mutterings like ends of summer storms —

the rain stops
the livid cloud grinds south
                and Gerda picking raspberries
beside me — just a child when
British bombers hurled death from the sky
brings her brimming hands to touch me

heavy, sweet
the fruit falls from her purple fingers
into mine.

MONTREAL FROM ST. CATHERINE'S LOCK, ST. LAWRENCE SEAWAY.

This is the place
we saw the one-legged man fishing
balancing his elbow crutch in shallows
while the current tore round his single leg
lifting the water against his wader.
Taken off balance he braced himself
against the muddy bank where a few rushes still flowered,
pulling in on his spinning reel
a big grey trout.

In summer I used to come here — out from the city
to paint the rapids and the Mountain from the trailer park.
Butter-and-eggs and phlox rising above the rough grass
recalled barbecues smoking
and children darting like water insects
on the edge of the rapids.
All gone, all gone, but the Sunday fisherman.

Once we came back in January
knowing it was the last time.
From the dead trailer park
it was a landscape without colour
a pallette of grey and black would have done it —
ice islands whaled to the surface
loud water scurried through drowned branches, stones,
where the fisherman had stood.

Shivering we watched steam rolling far out
over ridge after ridge of compacted ice
seagulls wheeling above the water
repeating the waves pattern — diving
perpetually rising into clearer air
as they scavenged for food in churned grey garbage
finding only
black winter fish, a dead man's hand.
I think of them now I'm exiled
wheeling through unresting satisfactions
never migrating.

INTERIORS

I enter the municipal greenhouse
where mop-headed chrysanthemums
stand to attention.

A loudly running stream
cuts through their banks
of white, yellow, plum.

A real rustic wellhead
unwinds its bucket
under waterfalls of flowers.

In the pool
black and vermillion carp
flick lustrous bony tails.

Black labels
proclaim the chrysanthemums' names:
Orpheus, Christmas Gold and Brandywine,

Gypsy Torch, and Sunny Monday —
flowers cascade
even from the cornices

the shaggiest chrysanthemums
turn back pale inner petals —
distillations of their outer colours

tensely they lean against their stakes
and green string — familiars
waiting for their masters.

Stand back, Orchid Beauty,
Flesh-coloured Decor,
White Spider, and Bronzitos!

And you, beside the Roman
bath, Tangerine-coloured Tuneful —
why do you smell of dander — and shudder?

THE ANATOMIST

Remember, Doctor Anxious said
that this was once a man.

The cadaver was grey
thick rubber with sunken mouth
and we wore white
for the dissection.
We were flippant in the mediastinum
levering through the ribs' bars
squeezing solid bags of lungs.

Arteries
nerve-strings, muscles,
bones, rattled our tongues
serpents slipped from omentums
secrets spilled
from liver and spleen
shreds straggled from
dry cheek plates
eyes yielded their jelly
and the stiff mouth which
once had kissed
revealed a skeleton leaf of nerves.

We left the heart
till last.
It was a livid
grotto of four chambers
and gothic fan vaulting —
and hard as a stone.

Tonight, under the thrusting
beat of your heart,
under the merciless
pump of love
I'll remember
what men become.

RELAX AND ENJOY IT

The sharp sun
cuts out the boundaries
of my geography
the edges are marked
with black

But the gallows crane
is daffodil yellow
and over the drilled-out
graves of old houses
gibbets balance in
plaid patterns.

And what I want to say is
we've only ourselves
to hang.

QUEBEC PAINTERS

Yesterday was a Cosgrove day:
haze on a few beige paper leaves,
grass, sea-grey,
fat squirrels
starlings under the eaves

Last night — snow
today
a Jean-Paul Lemieux day:
white flat fields
people and buildings
mauve and grey
or black

buildings
either like
rocks
or elaborate
sheds   some
ready to fall

some tiered
for winged nuns

our painters see life
through powdered
glasses
whether it's bowls
and terra-cotta apples
or faces like candled
eggs
on bodies also eggs
or dolls with smaller dolls inside.

CIRCLING

Marriage is being,
is being sat on
by a fat woman
caught
in the cleft of her
buttocks.

Marriage makes you into
a beetle
with legs flagellating
and going nowhere
on its back.

Marriage is the
ball-bearing
that keeps you roaring on to
death when you would
rather wait

to hear the / silence when
the earth rolls over
the crackle when / the trilliums
open.

Are worlds turning
flowers crackling
better known
from inside / body's prison?

or does the globe
swing in cracks
of thunder
not of flesh?

CASTING OFF — THORNHILL AVENUE, MONTREAL.

I lay at anchor in my garden
looking up through the leaves of the elm at the oriole
flashing like a buoy
in the mounting waves
of the sky where clouds streamed before the wind
and here amongst bees and evening primroses was calm
and I knew it couldn't last because nothing one loves
    ever does
but even change is better than loss

so I lay and thought of Penelope
and the weaving I would do that day
of words to cover words to cover feelings
because nothing one loves can survive
being seen or written because it changes
and perhaps to something better
and the past can never return
even the past of an old house
here, where the fire station was once a quarry
and these six houses stood close to the edge
and were close to the edge for the time I was there
before I slipped my cable
before I fell over.

2

JUST VISITING

FISHING FOR THE INUIT SEA GODDESS

I walk the six
museum cases and
I stand here looking in,
an eye blot, a mysterious
full moon swimming her outer sky.

She, inside, sprawled on a rock
in balloon splendour, looks out.
I read here that the
kitten clinging to her
with a sharp hungry face
half her size and angry
is her father . . .
no, never grown bigger
than a ten year old child.

In the second case
the goddess drifts in state
born high by the great turtle her servant.
The Narwhale, her protector, swims above
probing the future with his long spike,
missing perhaps the horse body
I feel he ought to have.

In the next case
she's unplaited her hair
brought to the surface
by a broken taboo.
Take warning from the
square mouth of rage
the bare oblong teeth.

Furiously she rends
the sea's skin with heaving
flipper waves while
her angry hair grows longer, longer
serpents
twisting all round her
reaching out for sinners.
Paddle hard, Inuit,

keep to shore, beach the canoe,
until she braids her punishing hair
up tight again.

The gentle goddess
carved from a walrus tooth
is a genial ivory smelt.
She beams, she's like spring ice
floating and melting
seeking her dog-faced husband.

But in the next case
her head juts from
a smooth, no-necked
blimp body,
walrus-flippered and
fish-tailed, with
impersonal dot eyes
in a triangular face
holding onto mine though
her new-braided hair
reassures me.

I read: when
she married the dog,
her father cut off
her fingers.

The joints became
fiord seals, bearded seals,
walruses: her thumb a bear . . .
all as much like her
as the dog-children
from her womb.

Shall I, trailing old myth
like seaweed,
and wearing a seal skin,
join her herd
casting my net for a prophecy?

Now she braids her hair
for the halcyons
and sings, while
I, in my seal disguise,
hot and stinking
in alien fur and blubber,
hear her song through
new round ears.

I throw
my harpoon of learning
my net of words
arching over the ice.
The wide seine glitters
catching animals, spirits, her familiars,
wriggling at my feet.

Now I throw the seine
over the last case.

She lies purring
in new shapes:
a bristling bear, a white wolf,
owl, sea-lion, loon,
or pillars of light
across the Northern stars;
an icy torrent
a trickle of water . . .

She escapes me.

DISTANCES
OUTDOOR SCULPTURE EXHIBITION OF
HENRY MOORE

From here
they are a line of old dinosaurs
seals walking
moving apart and together

As I approach
each takes a proper
distance from the other.

And this old curled figure
hunched against Pompei's
lover with its
baby poised between its legs
is a worn seashell mother
whose baby is a clam
just born
and reaching for the nipple

as you reach through distances
to touch.

JUST VISITING

Here, where
the sun's a warrior
light finds a hard way

into barricaded rooms
where shutters make
perpetual shadow.

Din stabs
walls and buffers
and the hi-fi across the

sky-blue pool
blows my gauzy-curtained
mind with hard rock airs.

Radios scream about sales and murders
a folksy voice selling Burdines
says he's hibernated

his pool. Here, where you may be
lonely, every man cries, "Ha ya doin'?"
Every woman, shrilling, "Hi!"

Here, where a stick
shoved into the melon mound
roots in the rain

here, the warrior sun
dips lower, piercing deeper
because it's winter.

And a parked car across the street
reflects from a pastel shell
a banner of buff light

and New Year's Eve on Ponce de Leon
death slams shut the
the Southbound

and occulting police lights
make shining balls of
hanging Christmas faces

and sirens echo the Spinners
playing here only last week.
And the man

squatting beside the wrapped
form in the road
is just visiting.

BLACK HOLE

A single leg
noded like a grass stem
supports all

The flamingo's eye
looks out from his round head
folded back
on an ampersand neck
and a sad feather-whorled
seashell body
a yellow glass eye
with a black hole
in the centre

Another flamingo
a salmon-painted swan with upper
wing plumes tattered pink
and fluttering orange tail
lies on the grass
eyes closed

Another flamingo
groans and spreads
hanging black curtains
and thrusts
a crab-claw bill
with buff band
yellowed like an old kid glove
into its back.
It blinks twice, shuts its eyes
twisting into the economical space
of an Etrog sculpture.

Another flamingo
looks into the first flamingo's eye.
It braces one leg sideways
needing this
quivering guy wire
to hold the world
still.

*OUTAGE AT KEY BISCAYNE

A seagull with a yellow eye
awaits bread
Europeans with a new baby
talking about Russia
send shrimp-naked children
into the sea
an illegal
miniature poodle
quivers beneath a beach chair
"Mona!" cries its fat mistress
as it pirouettes out
chasing a rubber mouse
a girl walks the foam line
the tape deck growing from her
liver spewing country music
"I knew all the great artists,"
says the man like an ostrich
"My grandfather travelled from Norway
to Paris for the Rite of Spring."
The blond mother of the
baby tourniquets her belly
with a purple stretch bikini.

Dark young men throw
frisbees, handstand on oil cans,
shouting Spanish
casuarinas from the antipodes
their sprays dipped in scarlet
rattle wounding burrs to
the needled ground
sea-oxeye primps and vetches
sprawl the dunes
and the Goodyear blimp parts
the thick plastic sky
a sign admonishes
It is Unlawful to Pick Sea-oats
or Walk on the Dunes.

A pale butterfly kite
skitters up from the
hand of a child
collides with a streamered bandit
a paper portuguese man-o-war.

The plangent radio voice
glissandos to a halt —
then races — bursts
out with the assassin's shot —
anticipates a dirge —
unheard.

*Note: In Florida, a power failure is called an "outage".
        President Reagan was shot March 30 1981.

ST. HELIER, JERSEY, CHANNEL ISLANDS.

A more unlikely place to smell antiquity
I can't imagine: vulgar crowded island,
provincial, sheltering millionaires
in granite strongboxes.

I walked out over the causeway at low tide
from St. Helier to Elizabeth Castle; meandered
over the grassy forecourts, examined the old
stables and armories, the empty
gunports, which once showed black stumps
of cannon, thrown by the Germans at Liberation
onto the rocks below. I examined the new tableaux,
authentically costumed wax figures
in a stance of embarrassment.
I read: Charles the second, when Prince of Wales,
was here as a fugitive, and was entertained
by Phillip de Carteret — a name like Justin de Villeneuve,
but in this case, quite real, quite proper. But
where was the smell, the smell of
antiquity.

I smelt it a moment at La Houghue Bie,
extraordinary inland hump,
crowned with two
contiguous chapels. Under the hill — stoop and
enter the ancient, holy, tomb — there smell antiquity:
it was bone-dry, knife-dry, when they accidentally found it
had been looted, of course, some
centuries before, but there remain
cup-marks — wizards' books —
chipped out of the stone.

So I went out over the far causeway
(built in the nineteenth
century, from the castle on l'Islet)
to Saint Helier's sharp eyrie.

The martyr saint,
butchered by Norse pirates,
had been an embarrassment to his Bishop,
Marculf;
a tiresome fellow,
living on his pinnacle
of sharp, unfriendly rock (hardly
even tufted with warm grass).
He often starved.
On calm days he paddled
a corracle to shore.
Island men fed him,
awed by his twig limbs
and calm eyes
grey as the winter sea.

I climbed the steep track
to the place above the reach of the spray.
I felt it like a physical blow,
high on the needle rock, as I
tightly held a tuft of warm sea pinks.
I saw the Norsemen's prows;
I knew the biting sword,
I felt the martyr there —
and all the community of Iona — there.

And I smelt the odour of antiquity.

ZERO FAHRENHEIT

Walking in the hard
sunshine I saw
steam boiling twenty
feet above the lake
the huge white chimney
from the heating plant
breathing a column of
life as I mounted the
slope to the patient's centre

Cheery nurses some
dressed in pink
ran up and down
with files
carrying lives
lightly to doctors
I suppose there must have been
music — the faces
of women waiting were blank
not listening
only their eyes moved
shifting like the steam
I'd seen
blowing away from the heating plant
and swept the waiting room
for others brought down like themselves
by inner disaster —
steaming life gone mad

And we followed one another
from test to test —
when I left the cold bit my face —
what bliss to feel it
reprieved as I was
warm, whole and pulsing
and I breathed a column
of life into the frost
and watched it.

AT BIRLING GAP

I sit in a sea-scooped hollow
under the cliff with a green cap
and a white-faced bird
swings over long flats of seaweed
beyond the shimmering islands.

There in the distance
the seventh sister fades
and I'm disappearing too
as I sit in the cold mother hand of the cliff.

That child there, with the blue shrimping net
ballooning out behind her as if it would lift
her into the sky
she might be me —
she skips in and out
of white lines of waves
and brings me a bunch of slippery sea grapes
with an embryo fish inside each brown egg.

I run my hand along a grey line
in the shining cliff
and watch her run from
my lair of flint
to foaming water line.

REGATTA

Imagine a Regatta beside a prison. At night in the harbour
the boats are held in a noose of concrete. On the broad dock
the dinghies in cradles, stockaded with masts

close, floating in a moat of green grass, the prison
the swivelling guns giving the guards a joyride. The
prisoners never seeing the sailors. Nor the sailors the
prisoners. Perhaps there are no prisoners and the vast
walls stand only to support the guns and the guards

On the day the regatta is over, little grey boats like
ducks file past the concrete shrilling their
whistles. All the sirens are blowing. All the flags are
standing out stiff in the wind.

The prison stays the same; guns the same; towers the same;
guards the same.

We sailors are leaving.
We think we are leaving the prison behind.

3

A HINGE OF SPRING

SILVER

A snow storm on April the twenty-seventh
covered the grass with despair
though I'm told that minerals
caught by the flakes splashing down on the still cold earth
start flower roots growing.
Next day the Russian olive planted
just last year and three feet high
still showing only scabs of buds
was alive with red enameled and spotted insects —
scores of ladybirds
encrusting the twigs where they toiled.

They were mating
each bug's head with two white spectacled eyes, teetering
in the struggle to mount another
with black and scarlet armour lifted
and dark gauzy wings whirring the air underneath
for balance so the 6 thread legs could cling.
And in the sun they seemed to clatter and sing
and every leaf of the olive tree stirred
silver in its scaly bud.

DAYS OUT

Montreal basks in shirt-sleeved April sun
returned exile I drink
in an outdoor bar on Mackay Street
then go by metro to buy sandals
at the Real Enrico Shoe Shop.

The machinery of shoe mending's gone
no rattling lathes and stacks
of finished bagged lost shoes —
though the blonde behind the counter bosses the show
as always: "not many people remember Enrico,"
(but I do) "Etore owns the store now,"
and Etore's son
fits children
old ladies, nurses and the rich.

"Harya, Mrs. Warken, is it you?"
Etore himself — almost himself — white hair is new —
checked sports coat, tie, grey flannels,
who used to wear black pants, white shirt sleeves.
Fresh Etore, who, when asked, "Do you dye?"
once replied, "We all die, young lady!"
now sits down beside me, time to kill:
"I'm in town for the day. Live North of here
at Lakeview. Put Mother in the hospital there —
she's got the sugar, needs a special diet . . .
Na-a-a, I'm in the shoe business
all my life.
Shoes is all I know.
Folks at Lakeview, all they know
is drinking."

"How's Fred?" I ask, remembering
the dog
"Fearless Fred, I call him. Loved
the shop. Liked a day out though — went
to the plush apartments on de Maisonneuve.
Fred don't seem to know his proper place.
He's nine now — a city dog —
don't like the sissy country."

Me neither, Fred.

A TASTE OF PURDY

Seventeen years
in a mattress factory!
Oh Al! you've got to be kidding!

A March Hare
with straw in his ears
and a whiskery smirk

in a mattress factory!
Horsehair or springs?
Was time's tired ticking
embroidered roses or stripes?

There are so many gigs
a man may dance that if he
twangs springs in a mattress
factory there must be coherence.

Between pallet and poet
a need and a marriage.

HOME THOUGHTS FROM AT HOME — LAKE ST. LOUIS, QUEBEC.

It's April! They
have gone to Jamaica
there they may pleach
bent sermons saying why
they need the heat, the tattered palms
lascivious oleander's mouth and carmine
rum-sweet sunsets

Keep it! Today
the wind makes the lake a
hard blue beach
for a white-capped ocean of sky
and a screeching blackbird drops his alms
from the resinous quills of a Northern pine
on beer bottles   cold in snow setts.

AN OLD MAN'S SPRING — SAANICH PENINSULA, B.C.

Ignore the blue,
green, yellow of the
view to see the brown
Spring. The two ducks
frozen in take-off
stand the same
wings spread
against the dark primulas and
the sprouts of new
rose leaves and red
palm frond shoots
of peonies.

Beyond, the contained sea and
threat of islands;
shade of far peaks
repeats tranquility
of an old shell
or an old wife, new known.
And if, far beyond,
a full rigid peak
glistens unworldly
with new-born colours
white, pink, blue
it reminds me only of shadows
of shadows.

BURSTING THE COCOON

In the cocoon, sister,
it is grey
a parchment sky sifts light
like a ribbed milkweed's pod
a tough skin, a caul,
my elbow and knee
mar its smooth surface

bulging it like
the gibous wave of a
snake's swallowed meal
or Dizzy Gillespie's
bellows cheek
leaking the dark blues.
In the cocoon, sister

we dream:
once the sun shone
under the long seawall
where the stunted poplars
wrung their leaves
all wriggling white with salt
and hawk moth larvae chewed.

We picked glue-footed
caterpillars to keep in jam jars
and while we slept
they spun their winding sheets
and all by morning were
cetaceous eggs, or Lot's
wives solid as bolsters

and in the cocoon
the folded moths
dreamed pleated wings
in oleander colours
purple and pink,
and the new life's
first flight

I heard them twittering
in their paper wombs
with voices just like ours
as we flutter back and forth
within our taut membrane
of sky, dreaming, sisters, dreaming
of the bursting.

WE ARE WEEDS

We are weeds
            our seed
needs only a murmur
of rain, a signal
            of sun

      not for us
the special pot
the warmed bed
the brown cover

      we are not
the kept plants whose
sumptuous blooms are
      seducers of bees
and hummingbirds' playthings

      we spread
our small flowers
for carrion flies

      we want
the earth!
      Poison us!
Break us!

But here by the hedge
in the gravel
stars will appear
            for
white
is our colour.

A HINGE OF SPRING

A blazing bird melted a twig's
white cover — then there's another

what can a cardinal want with winter
warming the snow and rock-grey grass?

cold binoculars fog over
I rub and the birds jump huge in the centre
of the round theatre below my birdfeeder

the red male observes the armoured pigeons
khaki sparrows, spike-furred squirrels

and swivels a princely black cat's face
and quietly drops in the trodden circle
stands refulgent and splendid

startling the ruck he makes this country
in crimson majesty blesses our garden
and hinges spring open.

LA BÊTE

Like every Fall
this is the beginning
of the first year of my life.

Previous lives
trail me like old snake skins
rattling.

Outside my window orange leaves
fly to the west;
branches of trees

twist in webs
concealing the Beast's castle.
In previous lives I

prowled the high thorn hedge
guarding the Beauty's palace;
medallioned with blood

my hands parted the brambles.
I am outside my window
and gloved with the patterned

armour of age
I seize the green spikes.
Proceed first year of my life.

4

IS IT REALLY LOVE

DROUGHT

for my mother

In the end the wide window
narrowed. It became a slit for wanting
nothing — except the wide sea's swinging

the restless sea of suffocating
sadness, heavily splashing,
fog-bearing, having all the qualities of
rain — but one:

the sea can't bring the cracked earth
to bloom, then harvest,
by frilling its wrinkled skin, or if it did
the salt rime

would first encrust then crystalize
the heart-shaped leaves,
soft-furrowed green, and the lion faces
of caterpillars

who, when caught and put in a box
make silver chrysalises
during the night, unseen, awaiting
the waiting's end.

THE PASSENGER'S SEAT

They mended her face
but the eye shrivelled up
to lie dead in the socket

so they made it a casket
morbidezza on plastic
eye-shaped to mask it

with iris coloured like sunny
green seawater, perfectly
matching, or nearly, the real eye

and the shrunk eye shut
in elliptical night
remembered the day

inside its prison
it tried to swivel
but the inelastic

pretty plastic
held to its groove
the eye could not move

immured in the dark
yearning for light
it could not cry!

The false disc smiled but it
could not see. No, it could not see —
and of course — nor could she.

SEASIDE LOVESONG

Drawn by
its strobe lights
its invitation
I thrust my finger
under the water
of a flashing tidal pool

Anemones
trail siren tendrils —
searching mouths
for living food

Shall I offer them
my finger?

A charged rod
activating iron
filings, my finger
sends to the tendrils
shrimps and tiny
crustaceans.

An anemone closes
tightly digesting
a caught shrimp.

The half-shrimp
struggles. No more
ripples. Predator
and prey are one.

My finger
is a tendril
my arm
entwines you

I am an anemone
I enclose you

Who will
digest who?

IS IT REALLY LOVE

Encapsulate love
    as an unidentified flying
Object — put it with
    its paraphernalia
Into a thin-skinned
    cigar-shaped container.

Shoot that into orbit.

Think of it now at apogee
    as it darts slyly to the moon.
Does that lady who hears
    a dree singing and sees
a hundred portholes shining

Know that the portholes
    are punctures,
The light blazing
    is bleeding?

Scything the hemlocks the capsule
    crashes. There it hangs
limply, like an alarm clock over
    the boulders.

And where, oh where
    are the little green men?
        Singing Love's Old Sour Song again.

KILLED WHILE CLEANING
HIS GUN

The white faces
his children's faces
dull the quivering altar lilies

and the face of his wife is bare —
where no one looks
she balances her eyes.

Her face is bare
is bare and thin and white
caustic, as if burned with ice

Creaking with awe
and awkward pace, his friends,
the young pall bearers come

they sway from side to side
to make the distance more
measure a greater space
from font to burial place.

CITY LOVE

They are drilling a wound
in the street
but here   between
smooth walls
only the aluminum
chair arms quiver

The pigeons feed on cigarettes
and rancid
sandwiches and peck
on indoor-outdoor green —
after the dustbath
armoured-in-tortoiseshell
sparrows on the sill
of the chromium-surfaced pool
drink chlorinated water

A pincer-beaked fire-
breasted robin   raiding
plastic pots for prey
stretches to breaking point
a worm   and chomping
along its length
like an automatic knitter
mollifies and subdues it to
a pre-digested string

As the maceration
by the bird's bill
readies the worm
for eating   so
the pool's blank glitter
drill scream and hammering
sun's pressure
soften and unravel me
until
there's nothing but this
spasmodic thrilling
death after death
by drilling

5

SHADOWS

WARPING OUT

I felt my mother's heart beat and the beat
of another heart. The book in her hands
made a circle around me.
I was with her in a winged galleon
as we sailed out to visit the planets.

Her voice spun walls of mist
and dissolved them
till we sailed through and landed in a blue field
where beside a lake of bronze a princess
danced, her hat adazzle with jewels
and white unicorns came to drink
and drank up all the water until
the lake was a dirty puddle.
The princess began to glow and then
all that was left was an aura
and that faded to a shadow.
And my mother sighed.

Tell me another, I cried —

My mother said she was tired and wanted to rest —
she said she would read from the book
in exchange for my painting
a picture of the story.

I raced for my paints
and splashed the bright colours everywhere.
But the princess, the lake, escaped me.
All I could make out was the aura
and feel my mother's heartbeat.

HER ROOM IN PARIS

(after seeing the installation, "Likely Stories", by Vera
Frenkel at the Agnes Etherington Art Centre, Kingston.)

Her wig stuffed in a painted box and
rosy shutters, separate, leaning against
plaster splashed with pink. The stuffed
boudoir chair where everyone
views the video screen
on the dresser with the drawers
spilling a sharp blue boa over fans a wig and
opera tickets, the things we think
she loved — if we think she was

under the dresser I see the tape
deck's careful rules typed up
embalmed in plastic;
ignoring the postcards propped
on the mantel, coyly displaying brown
ruins of temples and women I
obediently pull the knob marked ON
push the button POWER
and punch the FORWARD square

A faint squawking like April geese
heralds quivering rainbows
(emblems of hope like the half-
concealing entrance curtain)
they flash to a fountain
pen in soft insincere
fingers furrowing the thick
receiving paper
Her Room in Paris

Colour — faces, wine, appear —
all Cornelia — all evangelical
even the bibulous friend
with the lover
talking of
Cornelia's novel . . .

In another incarnation
the CBC researcher introducing a
Program: *Our Lost Canadians*
propounds *The Secret
Life of Cornelia Lumsden*
last seen near Kingston
boarding a train —
had she a double
before disappearing?

Here in her room the bird
cage twists white bars above
the painters' colour charts
cornelian through pale mauve
and the silk scarves
purple, red,
yellow silk, the faded rose,
the brittle carnation which, lo,
is in the hand of Cornelia's

hatted friend on the mirror screen
lying above a drawer of needles
metal spools, cosmetics.
And those three suitcases
wait to be filled
and carted away.
And I sit on a three —
legged stool, Cinderella
in my own ashes.

WINTER

As you gaze into the seapool's depths
the flint lights are only sea-dazzle
and your head and hand make shadows
on yellow lawns of an underwater garden
where a mass of siren anemones
hungrily drift their crimson tendrils —
and you offer your hand to their strange caresses —
like Proserpina in the Vale of Enna.

You start at the roll of distant thunder
still poking your finger into purple dreams —
as greedy mouths seize you
and down you sink
while iron tires roar through rock and seaweed
and flint lights spark from Pluto's chariot wheels.

ONCE AN IMAYO

In the tank
tropical fish flaunt
pale bodies
flickering shadows
of mauve and pink

and you know she's one too
that other
who sinks through glass
and greets the gods
with blinding colours

while you wait for her here in weeds
fluttering your antennae
like thin musical saws
signalling
from amongst skulls

but she cruises
the tank's green forests
looking out through
reversed bowls
of fishes eyes

and still her fish-mouthed
opening and shutting
invites you in and strains
you out.

PEEPHOLES 1 — GLIMPSE

The shower has left
one round puddle
a polished silver moon
against a sky
of damp black asphalt

like its mother moon
the puddle changes —

streamers of white
cross its surface
cockades and banners
from the pale ether
on a sunlit screen

but when a grey blanket
draws across the sun
the puddle shrinks
into the black
base of the city.

PEEPHOLES 2 — WRITING FICTION

It was called a Camera Obscura —
just a square room, standing alone
no windows, black curtains screening the entrance
and exit, the walls black except for one.

This pavillion was an illusion:
the illustration of a scientific principle,
light which enters a small lens
in the wall of a darkened box
projects and reverses an image of the outside world
oh, just the bit you can see through the hole
onto a white screen behind.

So I went inside.
The front wall was —
well, first let me tell you about the back wall.
The back wall was white — at least, at the edge,
near the corner — I lit my hand with the cone
of light beamed from the hole in the front wall.
My hand looked the same — no extra colours,
no people walking on a sky of grass. You see the —
the back wall was —

— an extraordinary panorama
of colour — blue lake — white
pavilions, a bank of purple
and pink petunias, enamelled
green plum trees, and people
standing on their heads,
legs criss-crossing on pale grey ceilings — everything
wrong way up.

I applied my eye to the hole
in the front wall
and looked out.
I jerked my eye away.
Things looked too strange
the right way up.

SHADOW OF ICARUS' WING — FOR JON

She remembered these times
when a black
white-blazed cat
shivered their lives
at a wild stream
flashing between brown
sticks and rocks
with black
and purple shadows.

She remembered him again
at two years old
stretching appealing hands
between the playpen's
bars
begging to be free
and how she let him out
saying his will
would be her death —
his father said,
"Don't let him fall!" . . .
so, crying and falling,
he jerked through childhood —

to school and college
and after McGill,
editor of a trade magazine,
becoming expert in boots and shoes, but
craving romance and fame.
Writing for bread
to Vancouver — where
rhododendrons in Spring
flaunted crimson passion in his face,
and the pawky broom,
yellow for philosophy
laid a scented trail.
Now he wrote of lumber
and said this was where he'd die.

Then he remembered
piebald rabbits
and cuddling together
until she became
shrunken, changed,
so he tried to forget her
becoming yet more lover
of wilderness — death.

And he, who had longed to escape
shut himself in a prison of work —
new bars stretched away —
away, like a man's long sighting
through a glass darkly
towards its pinhole end.

So next to Santa Barbara
where he nose-thumbed vicariously
dodging the martyrs
and shirkers of the draft
enjoying heady sixties riots
and a bank burning
making money flow
till money became the touchstone.

And he saw himself succeed
in a valley of mirrors stretching away
each image smaller
than the last.

And he remembered
early Vancouver days —
when he still loved her
when he netted the shallows
of Dead Man's Bay
for life-giving fish —

the houseboat in Vancouver Harbour
which swelled with plaintive airs
of folksong and guitar
smelled of Chinese ducks, and rang
with wok and cleaver —
then he remembered flying
late and early,
with a hand steady
on the plane's round wheel.

So in the seventies —
back to Vancouver and Simon Fraser,
and to Ottawa with high committees,
soaring still higher and higher
with a hand steady
on the round wheel.

Suddenly the hand was
trembling.
He plunged down through the
heavenly cirrus,
thrashed on the edge
of surflines,
never finding her, never found —

And his face appeared to her, just
beneath the surface,
reflection of a blotched
and ancient glass;
yet even then
his feet still felt the land,
and his heart still
held friends —
and sometimes his faint voice
quavered on a wire,
calling — but what was it saying?

Then his heavy feet
followed
his will
to the creek
and the wild stream
and the black
and purple shadows.

TANKA VERY MUCH

Those Japanese forms
of five seven five for a
thirty one total —
wire puzzles which click open
amazing thought in new spaces

A Hinge Of Spring is Patience Wheatley's first published collection of poetry, though her work has appeared in *The Antigonish Review*, *Mamashee*, *Contemporary Verse II*, *Quarry*, *Origins*, *Grain*, *Northern Light* and *Event*. She has also published a number of short stories, including the much-noted "Mr. Mackenzie King" in the anthology *Fiddlehead Greens* (Oberon, 1979).

The forty-three poems of *A Hinge Of Spring* are assured and confident in tone, and while their geographic locations are scattered there is little sense of the merely occasional. Wheatley's writing is characterized by a powerful imaginative intelligence in which literary associations and the response to immediate experience work together.

Patience Wheatley lives in Kingston, Ontario.

GOOSE LANE